travel journal

personal information

Name	Name
Address	Address
Telephone	Telephone
Mobile	Mobile
Email	Email
Emergency contact / next of kin	Emergency contact / next of kin
Important medical information	Important medical information
Blood group	Blood group
Optical prescription	Optical prescription
Passport number	Passport number
Driving licence number	Driving licence number
Bank (card loss number)	Bank (card loss number)
Insurance policy number	Insurance policy number
Insurance 24-hour helpline	Insurance 24-hour helpline
Travellers' cheque numbers	Travellers' cheque numbers

introduction

'A change is as good as rest.' There is nothing like contemplating travel to quicken the pulse. Whether you are planning a weekend in Venice or a fortnight's mountain trek in Nepal, a shopping break in New York or a week in Incan Peru, the prospect of experiencing new sights, sensations and cultures is irresistible for all but the most curmudgeonly stay-at-home.

Once you've decided that a trip is just what you need – where will you go? Do you want art and architecture, or a sun-drenched rest? Are food and wine top of your list, or action and adventure? Then of course, you need to take into account the wishes of the rest of the party. One olive-skinned friend who loves the beach and sun is married to a red-headed man who hates the sun and loves sport – a true travel challenge. One partner might like to be busy and stimulated while the other relishes the indolence of café life and people-watching. And for those who hate flights, the Channel Tunnel has made Europe easily accessible. A mere three hours' train ride from London, and you could be sitting with a bowl of *moules* in Paris.

Another element that plays quite a part in travel is fashion – places go in and out as much as the trouser flare. Once the Balearics were the height of chic (and indeed, some small lesser-known parts still are with the ultra-rich), now penguin-watching in Antarctica is a smart holiday option. India is perennially stylish, while Lisbon and Barcelona are popular with *cognoscenti*.

It may be too that timing plays a part in where you go. If you can, try and make sure you're not going to hit a major school holiday period – in France, for example, half-term is staggered throughout the whole of February. Meanwhile the middle part of the year is hurricane season in the Caribbean, and January in Nepal is when meningitis can rear its ugly head.

What all of this means is that when you've decided where you want to go – city, beach, forest, desert – you need to find out as much as possible to make the most of it. Tourist offices are a first stop, but they range in efficiency. Remember, their brochures are designed to sell. Word of mouth is very helpful – talk to friends who've already been. Get hold of some good travel guides and read up – what better excuse to browse in a travel book shop? (And yes, the one in *Notting Hill* does really exist!) Look at maps, surf the internet, treat yourself to a book or two – a visit to Italy would not be complete without a novel by E. M. Forster in your bag.

Decide how you want to get there. Is time of the essence? Then a plane is the answer. If time is on your side, take a meandering train, drive across Europe bed-and-breakfasting in chateaux on the way, or even go by boat. Where do you want to stay? Do you want a centrally placed top-of-the-range international hotel, or a charming family-run *pension* in a side street? What about a villa outside a city, but near enough to sample urban delights? Perhaps you feel less confident about booking it all independently, and you'd like a tailored package. Again, take recommendations when you go to an agent.

Budget too may play a part. Make sure you have a cushion – things can go wrong when you're away, and if you have calculated too tightly, you could find yourself in a hole. Apart from anything, you want to enjoy yourself. It would be a shame if you couldn't treat yourself to an unforgettable dinner at the Raffles Hotel in Singapore, or a silk suit in Bangkok, or a white-water rafting trip in New Zealand because you hadn't built in something for unforeseen extras. The cost of the trip is not just travel, accommodation and food. There are entrance fees to museums, visas, and all the other little expenditures that mount up. And before you leave, there is travel insurance to take out, visas and vaccinations to pay for, even the catsitter to pay.

But once the trip is organized and booked, it's time to get your bags ready. Try and travel light. It is rare these days that you will find yourself in a part of the world where you can't buy a substitute for something you've left behind. Take a small selection of clothes, which can cover a range of potential situations – smarter outfits if necessary, long sleeves and a scarf for women if going to a Muslim country, a tie for a man if needs be. Also be prepared for unexpected weather – pack one jumper even if you're going to a hot spot, as nights can be cool, or there may be a freak cold snap.

The key to a good trip is preparation. The more you feel in control of where you're going, and what you expect to find, the more you will get from the experience. Yes, culture shock does exist, but you can minimize its impact by feeling ready for the experience. Sometimes, the hardest part of travelling is actually coming home. You can feel so uplifted by what you've seen and done, or so moved and affected, that it's disheartening when everyone at home seems just the same as they ever were.

Your travel journal can help you with that – as a record of your trip, it can evoke memories of places and happenings that you don't want to let go. You can scribble down a note of a Prague church that was spellbinding, or an unforgettable meal of fresh Spanish fish that was pure Elizabeth David, or the address of a wonderful tailor in Hong Kong. You can slip in photographs to remind you of just how it was. Your own personal travel guide which you can refer to, expand and keep for ever.

Caroline Brandenburger

- Tickets

- Cash and
  travelers'
  checks

- Credit cards

- Address book

- Guidebook

- Vaccination details

- Medication—anything
  you take regularly and
  enough to cover your trip
  —also upset-stomach
  relief and so on

- Sun protection if
  appropriate for your
  destination

- Camera and film (if used)

- Money belt

- Copy of travel insurance
  documents

- Passport
  (for foreign travel)

- Visa (if necessary)

itinerary

Date

Destination

Depart

Arrive

Accommodation

Notes

Date

Destination

Depart

Arrive

Accommodation

Notes

Date

Destination

Depart

Arrive

Accommodation

Notes

Date

Destination

Depart

Arrive

Accommodation

Notes

museums, galleries and sights

museums, galleries and sights information

Attraction	Attraction
Address	Address
Directions	Directions
Admission	Admission
Opening hours	Opening hours
Highlights	Highlights
Attraction	Attraction
Address	Address
Directions	Directions
Admission	Admission
Opening hours	Opening hours
Highlights	Highlights

restaurants, bars and nightlife

restaurants, bars and nightlife information

Name

Address

Telephone

Opening hours

Directions

Comments

Name

Address

Telephone

Opening hours

Directions

Comments

Name

Address

Telephone

Opening hours

Directions

Comments

Name

Address

Telephone

Opening hours

Directions

Comments

Name

Address

Telephone

Opening hours

Directions

Comments

Name

Address

Telephone

Opening hours

Directions

Comments

shops and markets

shops and markets information

Name

Address

Telephone

Opening hours

Purchases

Amount spent

Name

Address

Telephone

Opening hours

Purchases

Amount spent

Name

Address

Telephone

Opening hours

Purchases

Amount spent

Name

Address

Telephone

Opening hours

Purchases

Amount spent

Name

Address

Telephone

Opening hours

Purchases

Amount spent

Name

Address

Telephone

Opening hours

Purchases

Amount spent

journal

So it is in travelling; a man must carry knowledge with him, if he would bring home knowledge

Samuel Johnson

itinerary

Date

Destination

Depart

Arrive

Accommodation

Notes

Date

Destination

Depart

Arrive

Accommodation

Notes

Date

Destination

Depart

Arrive

Accommodation

Notes

Date

Destination

Depart

Arrive

Accommodation

Notes

museums, galleries and sights

museums, galleries and sights information

Attraction

Address

Directions

Admission

Opening hours

Highlights

Attraction

Address

Directions

Admission

Opening hours

Highlights

Attraction

Address

Directions

Admission

Opening hours

Highlights

Attraction

Address

Directions

Admission

Opening hours

Highlights

restaurants, bars and nightlife

restaurants, bars and nightlife information

Name

Address

Telephone

Opening hours

Directions

Comments

Name

Address

Telephone

Opening hours

Directions

Comments

Name

Address

Telephone

Opening hours

Directions

Comments

Name

Address

Telephone

Opening hours

Directions

Comments

Name

Address

Telephone

Opening hours

Directions

Comments

Name

Address

Telephone

Opening hours

Directions

Comments

shops and markets

shops and markets information

Name

Address

Telephone

Opening hours

Purchases

Amount spent

Name

Address

Telephone

Opening hours

Purchases

Amount spent

Name

Address

Telephone

Opening hours

Purchases

Amount spent

Name

Address

Telephone

Opening hours

Purchases

Amount spent

Name

Address

Telephone

Opening hours

Purchases

Amount spent

Name

Address

Telephone

Opening hours

Purchases

Amount spent

journal

*One of the pleasantest things in the world is
going a journey; but I like to go by myself*

William Hazlitt

itinerary

Date

Destination

Depart

Arrive

Accommodation

Notes

Date

Destination

Depart

Arrive

Accommodation

Notes

Date

Destination

Depart

Arrive

Accommodation

Notes

Date

Destination

Depart

Arrive

Accommodation

Notes

museums, galleries and sights

museums, galleries and sights information

Attraction

Address

Directions

Admission

Opening hours

Highlights

Attraction

Address

Directions

Admission

Opening hours

Highlights

Attraction

Address

Directions

Admission

Opening hours

Highlights

Attraction

Address

Directions

Admission

Opening hours

Highlights

restaurants, bars and nightlife

restaurants, bars and nightlife information

Name

Address

Telephone

Opening hours

Directions

Comments

Name

Address

Telephone

Opening hours

Directions

Comments

Name

Address

Telephone

Opening hours

Directions

Comments

Name

Address

Telephone

Opening hours

Directions

Comments

Name

Address

Telephone

Opening hours

Directions

Comments

Name

Address

Telephone

Opening hours

Directions

Comments

shops and markets

shops and markets information

Name

Address

Telephone

Opening hours

Purchases

Amount spent

Name

Address

Telephone

Opening hours

Purchases

Amount spent

Name

Address

Telephone

Opening hours

Purchases

Amount spent

Name

Address

Telephone

Opening hours

Purchases

Amount spent

Name

Address

Telephone

Opening hours

Purchases

Amount spent

Name

Address

Telephone

Opening hours

Purchases

Amount spent

journal

The port from which I set out was, I think, that of the essential loneliness of my life

Henry James

itinerary

Date

Destination

Depart

Arrive

Accommodation

Notes

Date

Destination

Depart

Arrive

Accommodation

Notes

Date

Destination

Depart

Arrive

Accommodation

Notes

Date

Destination

Depart

Arrive

Accommodation

Notes

museums, galleries and sights

museums, galleries and sights information

Attraction

Attraction

Address

Address

Directions

Directions

Admission

Admission

Opening hours

Opening hours

Highlights

Highlights

Attraction

Attraction

Address

Address

Directions

Directions

Admission

Admission

Opening hours

Opening hours

Highlights

Highlights

restaurants, bars and nightlife

restaurants, bars and nightlife information

Name

Address

Telephone

Opening hours

Directions

Comments

Name

Address

Telephone

Opening hours

Directions

Comments

Name

Address

Telephone

Opening hours

Directions

Comments

Name

Address

Telephone

Opening hours

Directions

Comments

Name

Address

Telephone

Opening hours

Directions

Comments

Name

Address

Telephone

Opening hours

Directions

Comments

shops and markets

shops and markets information

Name	Name
Address	Address
Telephone	Telephone
Opening hours	Opening hours
Purchases	Purchases
Amount spent	Amount spent
Name	Name
Address	Address
Telephone	Telephone
Opening hours	Opening hours
Purchases	Purchases
Amount spent	Amount spent
Name	Name
Address	Address
Telephone	Telephone
Opening hours	Opening hours
Purchases	Purchases
Amount spent	Amount spent

journal

A traveller's chief aim should be to make men wiser and better

Jonathan Swift (*Gulliver's Travels*)

itinerary

Date

Destination

Depart

Arrive

Accommodation

Notes

Date

Destination

Depart

Arrive

Accommodation

Notes

Date

Destination

Depart

Arrive

Accommodation

Notes

Date

Destination

Depart

Arrive

Accommodation

Notes

museums, galleries and sights

museums, galleries and sights information

Attraction

Address

Directions

Admission

Opening hours

Highlights

Attraction

Address

Directions

Admission

Opening hours

Highlights

Attraction

Address

Directions

Admission

Opening hours

Highlights

Attraction

Address

Directions

Admission

Opening hours

Highlights

restaurants, bars and nightlife

restaurants, bars and nightlife information

Name

Address

Telephone

Opening hours

Directions

Comments

Name

Address

Telephone

Opening hours

Directions

Comments

 Name

Address

Telephone

Opening hours

Directions

Comments

Name

Address

Telephone

Opening hours

Directions

Comments

Name

Address

Telephone

Opening hours

Directions

Comments

Name

Address

Telephone

Opening hours

Directions

Comments

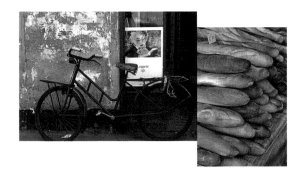

shops and markets

shops and markets information

Name

Address

Telephone

Opening hours

Purchases

Amount spent

Name

Address

Telephone

Opening hours

Purchases

Amount spent

Name

Address

Telephone

Opening hours

Purchases

Amount spent

Name

Address

Telephone

Opening hours

Purchases

Amount spent

Name

Address

Telephone

Opening hours

Purchases

Amount spent

Name

Address

Telephone

Opening hours

Purchases

Amount spent

journal

A man should know something of his own country too, before he goes abroad

Laurence Sterne

itinerary

Date	Date
Destination	Destination
Depart	Depart
Arrive	Arrive
Accommodation	Accommodation
Notes	Notes
Date	Date
Destination	Destination
Depart	Depart
Arrive	Arrive
Accommodation	Accommodation
Notes	Notes

museums, galleries and sights

museums, galleries and sights information

Attraction

Attraction

Address

Address

Directions

Directions

Admission

Admission

Opening hours

Opening hours

Highlights

Highlights

Attraction

Attraction

Address

Address

Directions

Directions

Admission

Admission

Opening hours

Opening hours

Highlights

Highlights

restaurants, bars and nightlife

restaurants, bars and nightlife information

Name

Address

Telephone

Opening hours

Directions

Comments

Name

Address

Telephone

Opening hours

Directions

Comments

Name

Address

Telephone

Opening hours

Directions

Comments

Name

Address

Telephone

Opening hours

Directions

Comments

Name

Address

Telephone

Opening hours

Directions

Comments

Name

Address

Telephone

Opening hours

Directions

Comments

shops and markets

shops and markets information

Name

Address

Telephone

Opening hours

Purchases

Amount spent

Name

Address

Telephone

Opening hours

Purchases

Amount spent

Name

Address

Telephone

Opening hours

Purchases

Amount spent

Name

Address

Telephone

Opening hours

Purchases

Amount spent

Name

Address

Telephone

Opening hours

Purchases

Amount spent

Name

Address

Telephone

Opening hours

Purchases

Amount spent

journal

It happen'd one day about noon going towards my boat, I was exceedingly surpriz'd with the print of a man's naked foot on the shore

Daniel Defoe (*Robinson Crusoe*)

clothing and shoe sizes

Women's dress sizes

UK/Australia	8	10	12	14	16	18	20
US/Canada	6	8	10	12	14	16	18
Continental Europe/Asia	36/38	38/40	40/42	42/44	44/46	46/48	48/50

Women's shoe sizes

UK	3$\frac{1}{2}$	4	4$\frac{1}{2}$	5	5$\frac{1}{2}$	6	6$\frac{1}{2}$	7	7$\frac{1}{2}$	8	8$\frac{1}{2}$
US/Canada/Australia	5	5$\frac{1}{2}$	6	6$\frac{1}{2}$	7	7$\frac{1}{2}$	8	8$\frac{1}{2}$	9	9$\frac{1}{2}$	10
Continental Europe/Asia	36	36$\frac{1}{2}$	37	38	38$\frac{1}{2}$	39	39$\frac{1}{2}$	40	41	42	42$\frac{1}{2}$

Men's suit sizes

UK/US/Canada	34	35	36	37	38	39	40	41	42
Continental Europe/Asia	44	45	46	47	48	49	50	52	52
Australia	12	14	16	18	20	22	24	26	28

Men's collar sizes

UK/US/Canada	14	14$\frac{1}{2}$	15	15$\frac{1}{2}$	16	16$\frac{1}{2}$	17	17$\frac{1}{2}$	18
Continental Europe/Australia/Asia	36	37	38	39	41	42	43	44	45

Men's shoe sizes

UK/Australia	6	7	8	9	10	11	12
US/Canada	7	8	9	10	11	12	13
Continental Europe/Asia	40	41	42	43	44$\frac{1}{2}$	46	47

weights, measures and temperatures

Length	Weight	Volume	°Fahrenheit	°Celsius
1 centimetre = 0.39 inches	1 gram = 0.04 ounces	10 millilitres = 0.34 fl. ounces	0	−18
1 metre = 3.28 feet	100 grams = 3.53 ounces	1 litre = 1.06 quarts	32	0
1 kilometre = 0.62 miles	1 kilogram = 2.2 pounds	1 litre = 0.26 gallons	41	5
8 kilometres = 5 miles			50	10
	1 ounce = 28.3 grams	1 teaspoon = 5 millilitres	59	15
1 inch = 2.54 centimetres	$\frac{1}{2}$ pound = 226 grams	1 tablespoon = 15 millilitres	68	20
1 foot = 30.48 centimetres	1 pound = 0.45 kilogram	1 fluid ounce = 30 millilitres	86	30
1 yard = 0.91 metres		1 cup = 237 millilitres	100	38
1 mile = 1.61 kilometres		1 pint = 473 millilitres	104	40
		1 quart = 0.95 litres		

world currencies, dialing codes, and time zones

Country	Currency	Dialing code	Time (hours) based on EST	Time (hours) based on GMT
Afghanistan	Afghani	+ 93	+9½	+4 ½
Albania	Lek	+ 355	+6	+1
Algeria	Algerian dinar	+ 213	+6	+1
Andorra	Euro	+ 376	+6	+1
Angola	Kwanza	+ 244	+6	+1
Antigua and Barbuda	East Caribbean dollar	+ 1268	+1	−4
Argentina	Peso	+ 54	+2	−3
Armenia	Dram	+ 374	+9	+4
Australia	Australian dollar	+ 61	+12 to +15	+7 to +10
Austria	Euro	+ 43	+6	+1
Azerbaijan	Manat	+ 994	+10	+5
Bahamas	Bahamian dollar	+ 1242	EST	−5
Bahrain	Bahraini dinar	+ 973	+8	+3
Bangladesh	Taka	+ 880	+11	+6
Barbados	Barbadian dollar	+ 1246	+1	−4
Belarus	Belarusian rouble	+ 375	+7	+2
Belgium	Euro	+ 32	+6	+1
Belize	Belizean dollar	+ 501	−1	−6
Benin	West African franc	+ 229	+6	+1
Bermuda	Bermudian dollar	+ 1441	+1	−4
Bhutan	Ngultrum	+ 975	+11	+6
Bolivia	Boliviano	+ 591	+1	−4
Bosnia and Herzegovina	Mark	+ 387	+6	+1
Botswana	Pula	+ 267	+7	+2
Brazil	Real	+ 55	+1 to +2	−3 to −4
Brunei	Bruneian dollar	+ 673	+13	+8
Bulgaria	Lev	+ 359	+7	+2
Burkina Faso	West African franc	+ 226	+5	GMT
Burundi	Burundi franc	+ 257	+7	+2
Cambodia	Riel	+ 855	+12	+7
Cameroon	Central African franc	+ 237	+6	+1
Canada	Canadian dollar	+ 1	−3 to +1½	−3½ to −8
Central African Republic	Central African franc	+ 236	+6	+1
Chad	Central African franc	+ 235	+6	+1
Chile	Chilean peso	+ 56	+1	−4
China	Yuan	+ 86	+13	+8
Colombia	Colombian peso	+ 57	EST	−5
Congo	Central African franc	+ 242	+6	+1
Costa Rica	Costa Rican colón	+ 506	−1	−6
Croatia	Kuna	+ 385	+6	+1
Cuba	Cuban peso	+ 53	EST	−5
Cyprus	Euro	+ 357	+7	+2
Czech Republic	Koruna	+ 420	+6	+1
Democratic Republic of Congo	Congolese franc	+ 243	+6	+1
Denmark	Danish krone	+ 45	+6	+1
Djibouti	Djiboutian franc	+ 253	+8	+3
Dominica	East Caribbean dollar	+ 1767	+1	−4
Dominican Republic	Peso	+ 1809	+1	−4
Ecuador	Sucre	+ 593	EST	−5
Egypt	Egyptian pound	+ 20	+7	+2
El Salvador	Colón	+ 503	−1	−6
Estonia	Kroon	+ 372	+7	+2
Ethiopia	Birr	+ 251	+8	+3
Fiji	Fiji dollar	+ 679	+17	+12
Finland	Euro	+ 358	+7	+2
France	Euro	+ 33	+6	+1
Gabon	Central African franc	+ 241	+6	+1
Gambia	Dalasi	+ 220	+5	GMT
Georgia	Lari	+ 995	+9	+4
Germany	Euro	+ 49	+6	+1

Country	Currency	Dialing code	Time (hours) based on EST	Time (hours) based on GMT
Ghana	Cedi	+ 233	+5	GMT
Greece	Euro	+ 30	+7	+2
Greenland	Danish krone	+ 299	+1 to +4	−1 to −4
Grenada	East Caribbean dollar	+ 1473	+1	−4
Guatemala	Quetzal	+ 502	−1	−6
Guinea	Guinean franc	+ 224	+5	GMT
Guinea-Bissau	West African franc	+ 245	+5	GMT
Guyana	Guyana dollar	+ 592	+1	−4
Haiti	Gourde	+ 509	EST	−5
Honduras	Lempira	+ 504	−1	−6
Hungary	Forint	+ 36	+6	+1
Iceland	Króna	+ 354	+5	GMT
India	Indian rupee	+ 91	+10$\frac{1}{2}$	+5$\frac{1}{2}$
Indonesia	Rupiah	+ 62	+12 to +13	+7 to +8
Iran	Rial	+ 98	+8$\frac{1}{2}$	+3$\frac{1}{2}$
Iraq	Iraqi dinar	+ 964	+8	+3
Ireland	Euro	+ 353	+5	GMT
Israel	Shekel	+ 972	+7	+2
Italy	Euro	+ 39	+6	+1
Ivory Coast	West African franc	+ 225	+5	GMT
Jamaica	Jamaican dollar	+ 1876	EST	−5
Japan	Yen	+ 81	+14	+9
Jordan	Jordanian dinar	+ 962	+7	+2
Kazakhstan	Tenge	+ 7	+10 to +11	+5 to +6
Kenya	Kenya shilling	+ 254	+8	+3
Kuwait	Kuwaiti dinar	+ 965	+8	+3
Kyrgyzstan	Som	+ 996	+10	+5
Laos	Kip	+ 856	+12	+7
Latvia	Lats	+ 371	+7	+2
Lebanon	Lebanese pound	+ 961	+7	+2
Lesotho	Loti	+ 266	+7	+2
Liberia	Liberian dollar	+ 231	+5	GMT
Libya	Libyan dinar	+ 218	+6	+1
Leichtenstein	Swiss franc	+ 423	+6	+1
Lithuania	Litas	+ 370	+7	+2
Luxembourg	Euro	+ 352	+6	+1
Macedonia	Denar	+ 389	+6	+1
Madagascar	Malagasy franc	+ 261	+8	+3
Malawi	Kwacha	+ 265	+7	+2
Malaysia	Ringgit	+ 60	+13	+8
Maldives	Rufiyaa	+ 960	+10	+5
Mali	West African franc	+ 223	+5	GMT
Malta	Euro	+ 356	+6	+1
Mauritania	Ouguiya	+ 222	+5	GMT
Mauritius	Mauritian rupee	+ 230	+9	+4
Mexico	Mexican peso	+ 52	−1 to −2	−6 to −7
Moldova	Leu	+ 373	+7	+2
Monaco	Euro	+ 377	+6	+1
Mongolia	Tugrik	+ 976	+13	+8
Morocco	Moroccan dirham	+ 212	+5	GMT
Mozambique	Metical	+ 258	+7	+2
Myanmar	Kyat	+ 95	+11$\frac{1}{2}$	+6$\frac{1}{2}$
Namibia	Namibian dollar	+ 264	+7	+2
Nepal	Nepalese rupee	+ 977	+10$\frac{3}{4}$	+5$\frac{3}{4}$
Netherlands	Euro	+ 31	+6	+1
New Zealand	New Zealand dollar	+ 64	+17	+12
Nicaragua	Córdoba	+ 505	−1	−6
Niger	West African franc	+ 227	+6	+1
Nigeria	Naira	+ 234	+6	+1
North Korea	Won	+ 850	+14	+9
Norway	Norwegian krone	+ 47	+6	+1
Oman	Omani rial	+ 968	+9	+4

Country	Currency	Dialing code	Time (hours) based on EST	Time (hours) based on GMT
Pakistan	Pakistani rupee	+ 92	+10	+5
Palau	US dollar	+ 680	+14	+9
Panama	Balboa	+ 507	EST	−5
Papua New Guinea	Kina	+ 675	+15	+10
Paraguay	Guaraní	+ 595	+1	−4
Peru	Nuevo sol	+ 51	EST	−5
Philippines	Philippine peso	+ 63	+13	+8
Poland	Zloty	+ 48	+6	+1
Portugal	Euro	+ 351	+5	GMT
Puerto Rico	US dollar	+ 1787	+1	−4
Qatar	Qatari rial	+ 974	+8	+3
Romania	Leu	+ 40	+7	+2
Russian Federation	Ruble	+ 7	+7 to +17	+2 to +12
Rwanda	Rwandan franc	+ 250	+7	+2
St Kitts and Nevis	East Caribbean dollar	+ 1869	+1	−4
St Lucia	East Caribbean dollar	+ 1758	+1	−4
St Pierre and Miquelon	Euro	+ 508	+2	−3
St Vincent and the Grenadines	East Caribbean dollar	+ 1784	+1	−4
San Marino	Euro	+ 378	+6	+1
Saudi Arabia	Saudi riyal	+ 966	+8	+3
Senegal	West African franc	+ 221	+5	GMT
Seychelles	Seychelles rupee	+ 248	+9	+4
Sierra Leone	Leone	+ 232	+5	GMT
Singapore	Singapore dollar	+ 65	+13	+8
Slovakia	Euro	+ 421	+6	+1
Slovenia	Euro	+ 386	+6	+1
Solomon Islands	Solomon Islands dollar	+ 677	+16	+11
Somalia	Somali shilling	+ 252	+8	+3
South Africa	Rand	+ 27	+7	+2
South Korea	Won	+ 82	+14	+9
Spain	Euro	+ 34	+6	+1
Sri Lanka	Sri Lankan rupee	+ 94	+10½	+5½
Sudan	Sudanese pound	+ 249	+7	+2
Suriname	Suriname guilder	+ 597	+2	−3
Swaziland	Lilangeni	+ 268	+7	+2
Sweden	Swedish krona	+ 46	+6	+1
Switzerland	Swiss franc	+ 41	+6	+1
Syria	Syrian pound	+ 963	+7	+2
Taiwan	New Taiwan dollar	+ 886	+13	+8
Tajikistan	Tajik ruble	+ 7	+10	+5
Tanzania	Tanzanian shilling	+ 255	+8	+3
Thailand	Baht	+ 66	+12	+7
Togo	West African franc	+ 228	+5	GMT
Tonga	Pa'anga	+ 676	+18	+13
Trinidad and Tobago	Trinidad and Tobago dollar	+ 1868	+1	−4
Tunisia	Tunisian dinar	+ 216	+6	+1
Turkey	Turkish lira	+ 90	+7	+2
Turkmenistan	Manat	+ 993	+10	+5
Uganda	Ugandan shilling	+ 256	+8	+3
Ukraine	Hryvnia	+ 380	+7	+2
United Arab Emirates	Emirian dirham	+ 971	+9	+4
United Kingdom	Pound sterling	+ 44	+5	GMT
United States of America	US dollar	+ 1	EST to −5	−5 to −10
Uruguay	Uruguayan peso	+ 598	+2	−3
Uzbekistan	Som	+ 7	+10	+5
Venezuela	Bolivar	+ 58	+1	−4
Vietnam	Dong	+ 84	+12	+7
Western Samoa	Tala	+ 685	−6	−11
Yemen	Yemeni rial	+ 967	+8	+3
Yugoslavia	Yugoslav dinar	+ 381	+6	+1
Zambia	Kwacha	+ 260	+7	+2
Zimbabwe	Zimbabwean dollar	+ 263	+7	+2

First published in Great Britain in 2001
This edition published in 2011
by Ryland Peters & Small
20–21 Jockey's Fields
London WC1R 4BW

And in the USA
by Ryland Peters & Small, Inc.,
519 Broadway
5th Floor
New York, NY 10012

www.rylandpeters.com

10 9 8 7 6 5 4 3 2 1

ISBN 978 1 84975 090 5

Printed in China

Introduction by Caroline Brandenburger, former
editor of TRAVELLER magazine and editor of the
fifth and sixth editions of The Traveller's Handbook.

Jacket photography by Mark Scott

Photographs by Jan Baldwin, Catherine Brear,
Christopher Drake, Emilie Ekström, Scott Griffin,
Sarah Hepworth, Gabriella Le Grazie,
Brian Leonard, Robert Merrett, Andy Tough,
Simon Upton and Alan Williams.

Selected images from Waterside Living, Great
Escapes, Open Air Living and Wine Tastes Wine Styles,
all published by Ryland Peters & Small.